PIANO SOL[O]

Christmas Time

ISBN 0-7935-9642-4

HAL•LEONARD®
CORPORATION

7777 W. BLUEMOUND RD. P.O. BOX 13819 MILWAUKEE, WI 53213

Visit Hal Leonard Online at
www.halleonard.com

BRAZILIAN SLEIGH BELLS

By PERCY FAITH

Bright samba (♩ = 138)

THE CHRISTMAS SONG
(CHESTNUTS ROASTING ON AN OPEN FIRE)

Music and Lyric by MEL TORME
and ROBERT WELLS

Slowly, somewhat freely

THE CHIPMUNK SONG

Words and Music by
ROSS BAGDASARIAN

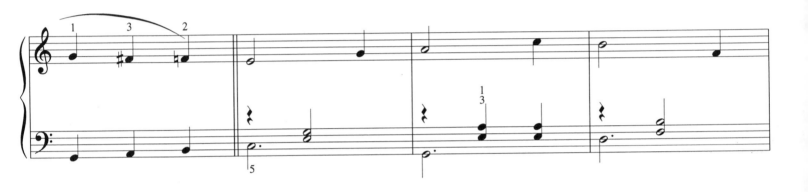

FELIZ NAVIDAD

Music and Lyrics by
JOSE FELICIANO

FROSTY THE SNOW MAN

Words and Music by STEVE NELSON
and JACK ROLLINS

With a swing

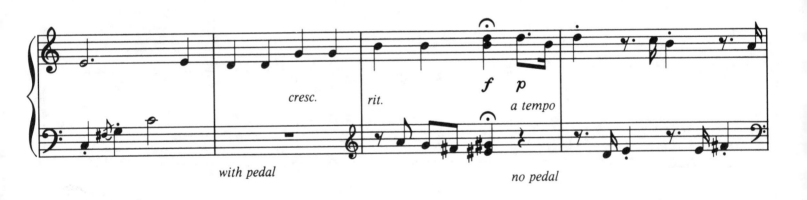

21

HAPPY HOLIDAY

from the Motion Picture Irving Berlin's HOLIDAY INN

Words and Music by
IRVING BERLIN

Slowly

GRANDMA GOT RUN OVER
BY A REINDEER

Words and Music by
RANDY BROOKS

HAPPY XMAS
(WAR IS OVER)

Words and Music by JOHN LENNON
and YOKO ONO

D.S. al Coda

CODA

(THERE'S NO PLACE LIKE)
HOME FOR THE HOLIDAYS

Words by AL STILLMAN
Music by ROBERT ALLEN

Medium bright country

A HOLLY JOLLY CHRISTMAS

Music and Lyrics by
JOHNNY MARKS

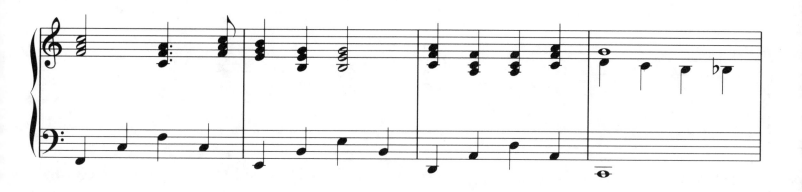

I SAW MOMMY KISSING SANTA CLAUS

Words and Music by
TOMMIE CONNOR

Moderately slow

I'LL BE HOME FOR CHRISTMAS

Words and Music by KIM GANNON
and WALTER KENT

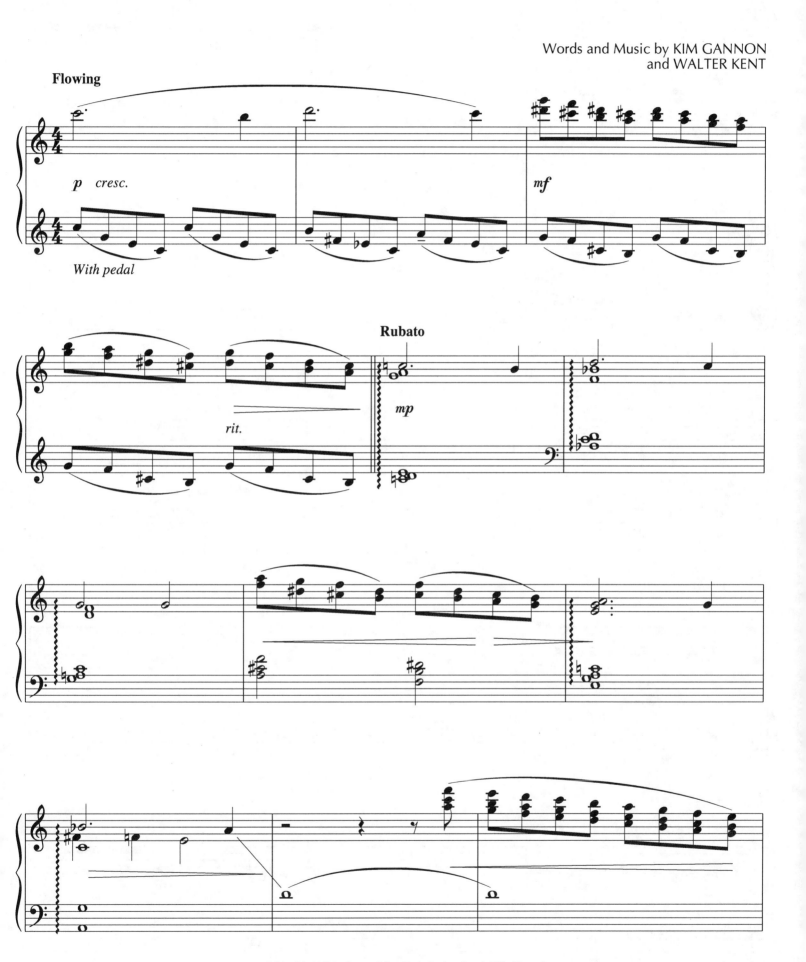

JINGLE-BELL ROCK

Words and Music by JOE BEAL
and JIM BOOTHE

A MARSHMALLOW WORLD

Words by CARL SIGMAN
Music by PETER DE ROSE

LET IT SNOW! LET IT SNOW! LET IT SNOW!

Words by SAMMY CAHN
Music by JULE STYNE

RUDOLPH THE RED-NOSED REINDEER

Music and Lyrics by
JOHNNY MARKS

SANTA BABY

By JOAN JAVITS,
PHIL SPRINGER and TONY SPRINGER

Moderately slow

SILVER BELLS
from the Paramount Picture THE LEMON DROP KID

Words and Music by JAY LIVINGSTON
and RAY EVANS

WONDERFUL CHRISTMASTIME

Words and Music by
McCARTNEY

Brightly

mf

With pedal

SNOWFALL

Lyrics by RUTH THORNHILL
Music by CLAUDE THORNHILL

Moderately slow

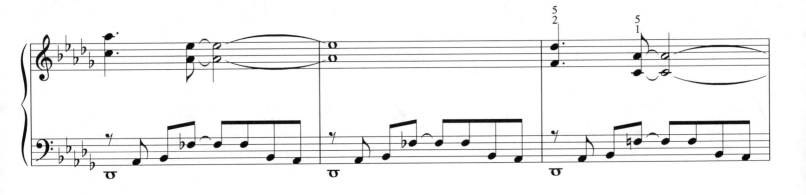

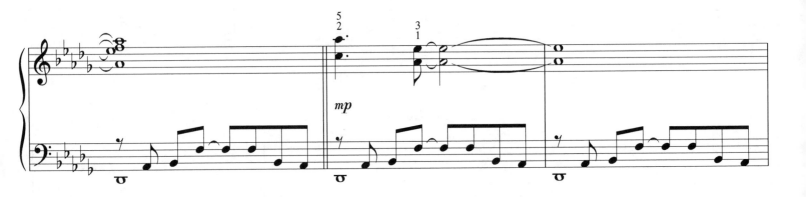